Maps to Bike Gettysburg
No. 5

The Ridges Extended Loop

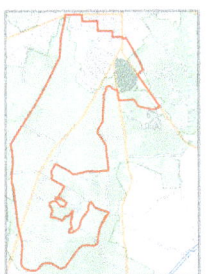

12.2 miles

Sue Thibodeau

A Companion Mini-Book for
Bicycling Gettysburg National Military Park

Maps to Bike Gettysburg No. 5:
The Ridges Extended Loop (12.2 miles)

Copyright © 2021 Sue Thibodeau

All Rights Reserved. No part of this publication may be reproduced, stored in an archival or retrieval system, distributed, or transmitted, in any form or by any means, including electronic or mechanical means, except in the case of brief quotations embodied in critical reviews and certain other non-commercial uses permitted by copyright law, without the prior written permission of the author.

Map Rendering Copyright © 2019 Sue Thibodeau
Map Data Copyright © OpenStreetMap contributors
www.openstreetmap.org/copyright
Liberation Sans Font Family, SIL Open Font License 1.1

Published by Civil War Cycling
154 Cobblestone Court Drive #110, Victor, NY 14564
Digital (PDF) maps sold separately at civilwarcycling.com

No Warranty. This book is distributed in the hope that it will be useful, but without any warranty, not even an implied warranty of merchantability or fitness for a particular purpose. Consult your doctor before bicycling. The directions provided in this book are for planning purposes only. Actual conditions (road, traffic, weather, or other events) may require you to adjust your route or actions, especially as needed to obey all laws, signs, alerts, and notices. If there are mistakes in this book, or if the park road network or policies have changed since this writing, it remains your responsibility always to act in ways that are safe, healthy, and legal. The author and publisher disclaim any and all liability. Please visit www.nps.gov/gett for official and up-to-date information about park roads, amenities, and policies.

ISBN 978-1-7326038-9-9 (pbk)

20210325-L7-1.6
First Printing

Maps to Bike Gettysburg No. 5: The Ridges Extended Loop (12.2 miles) is an educational mini-book that complements Civil War Cycling's 286-page comprehensive guidebook for a 23.8-mile tour:

civilwarcycling.com

Bicycling Gettysburg National Military Park: The Cyclist's Civil War Travel Guide
ISBN 978-1-7326038-0-6 (March 2019)

"Whether you're a cycling enthusiast, history buff, or both, Sue Thibodeau's *Bicycling Gettysburg National Military Park: The Cyclist's Civil War Travel Guide* is a must-have for your next visit to Gettysburg. In fact, this 286-page book is so chock-full of useful maps, photographs, and reference information about the battlefield's monuments, farm buildings, and areas of interest that it should be in the daypack of anybody touring the park and/or town of Gettysburg."

~ *Civil War Times*

"*Bicycling Gettysburg* is comprehensible to readers and riders of all ages and expertise... concise and readable for both aficionados and novices."

~ *Civil War Monitor*

"The best ways to truly see a battlefield are by walking and biking. And biking a battlefield such as Gettysburg provides a rush like no other. Sue has produced a valuable book about how to ride that most hallowed Civil War ground. A definite keeper."

~ John Banks, journalist, blogger, author

About the Author

Sue Thibodeau is a bicycling enthusiast, computer scientist, and former teacher. "Like a kid on a bike," she explores U.S. national military parks as a way to learn Civil War history. A graduate of Duke University, the University of Notre Dame, and the Rochester Institute of Technology, Sue publishes educational touring materials through Civil War Cycling.

She is the author of *Bicycling Gettysburg National Military Park* (2019); *Bicycling Antietam National Battlefield* (2020); and two forthcoming guidebooks, *Bicycling Chickamauga Battlefield* (2021) and *Bicycling Shiloh National Military Park* (2022).

About this Book

Maps to Bike Gettysburg No. 5: The Ridges Extended Loop provides color maps and turn-by-turn directions for a safe and educational, 12.2-mile park ride through the southern half of the Gettysburg battlefield. The route focuses specifically on Seminary and Cemetery Ridges, which were the main Confederate and Union battle lines on July 2-3, 1863. Designed for a lightweight ride, this book complements Civil War Cycling's more detailed and comprehensive guidebook, *Bicycling Gettysburg National Military Park*.

Maps to Bike Gettysburg No. 5 contains 16 detailed color maps with corresponding bicycle cue tables; 62 color photos; monument GPS points; and micro-histories for learning about the Battle of Gettysburg. It does not duplicate the guidebook's chapters on tour planning; orienteering  techniques; lengthy historical summaries; or monument descriptions for Route 1's 23.8-mile ride. It is an expanded print version of the Route 5 digital PDF map that is available at www.civilwarcycling.com/shop/.

Route 5 is a popular bike route that covers East Cemetery Hill, Seminary Ridge, Little Round Top, Devil's Den, Rose Woods, The Peach Orchard, and Cemetery Ridge. You will enjoy a winding, up-and-down ride—a 728' cumulative gain—through fields and woodlots, some of which are not on the park auto tour. Plan for a 3-hour ride with frequent stops to appreciate the beautiful landscape and some of the park's 1,300+ monuments. Route 5 limits exposure to busy roads; provides route-specific health and safety tips; identifies one-way roads; and notes the location of bicycle racks, water sources, restrooms, and picnic areas.

CONTENTS

Preface   9

1. **Getting Your Mind in Gear**   13
   The Battle of Gettysburg (1863)   13
   Gettysburg National Military Park   20
   The Ridges Extended Loop (No. 5)   22

2. **Let's Go! Bike Route 5**   27
   Route 5 Synopsis   27
   Similarities Between Routes 3–5   27
   Segment A (East Cemetery Hill)   28
   Segment F (Seminary Ridge)   32
   Segment G (Little Round Top)   40
   Segment H (Devil's Den)   44
   Segment J (The Peach Orchard)   48
   Segment K (Cemetery Ridge)   54
   Segment L (Return)   58

3. **What Next?**   61

Preface

For more than thirty years, and over many dozens of visits, I toured Gettysburg National Military Park by bus, car, and foot. In 2012, I toured the battlefield on a bicycle for the first time. The experience of learning American history while exploring park land on a bicycle is hard to describe, but if I had to pick one word, it would be "exhilarating." And yet it took four years to work out the kinks in my self-directed, solo tours. I was frustrated by one-way roads, incomplete or inaccurate maps, and not knowing how best to avoid town traffic. But I looked forward to every trip, and enjoyed them all.

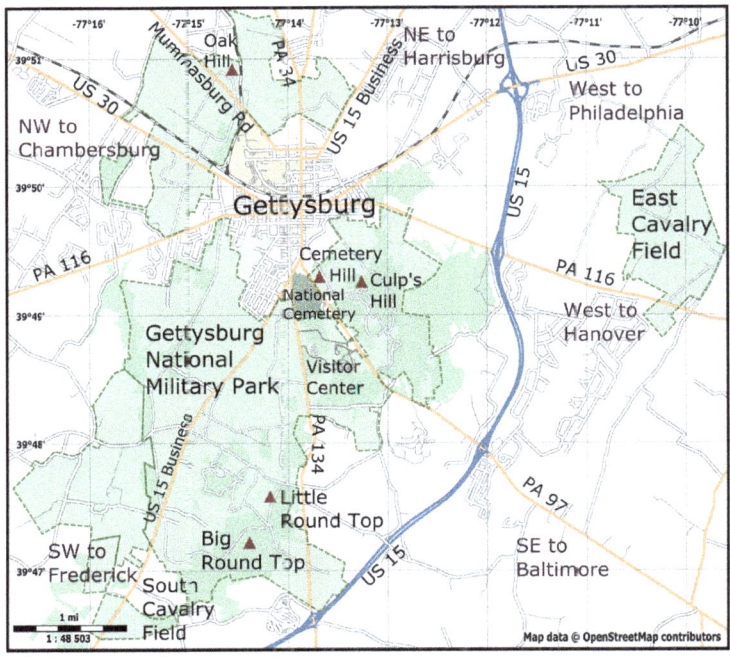

Map P.1. Gettysburg, Pennsylvania

Gettysburg National Military Park

Eventually, I learned what equipment to pack, what clothes to wear, and where to find convenient access to water, portable toilets, and shade for picnics. It was also challenging to know how best to sequence my visitation of monuments and within what general timeframe. I created my own maps (and guidebook) because I could not find any maps that met the needs of a bicycling historian. I hope that these maps help you to avoid the mistakes that I had made and that you can enjoy every minute of your battlefield tour.

In September 2018, I designed twelve digital PDF document maps that collectively define fourteen bicycle loops through the Gettysburg battlefield. The maps are available for secure online purchase and download from the Civil War Cycling website. Note: These digital files are not part of a GPS navigation system, and you will need Adobe's free PDF reader to view or print the maps and directions for your Gettysburg cycling tour.

Route #	Route Name	Miles
1	Full Day Loop	23.8
1b	Full Day Short Loop	11.5
2	Battle Day 1 Loop	10.5
3	Battle Days 2 & 3 Loop	17.0
3b	Battle Days 2 & 3 Short Loop	10.7
4	The Ridges Loop	9.0
5	**The Ridges Extended Loop**	**12.2**
6, 7	Culp's Hill Lower & Upper Loops	2.4 (ea)
8	Culp's Hill Double Loop	5.5
9–11	Devil's Den, The Wheatfield, and Little Round Top Loops	1.5–3.8
12	East Cavalry Field	5.2

Table of Gettysburg Bicycle Routes

For descriptions and details, visit Civil War Cycling at www.civilwarcycling.com/battlefields/gettysburg/routes/.

Given the popularity of the digital maps—and their appeal to bicyclists who want specifically themed historical rides over varying distances—I launched a paperback mini-book series in 2021 called *Maps to Bike Gettysburg*. Each mini-book is part of an independently usable set of educational publications. They are an expanded subset of Civil War Cycling's comprehensive guidebook for a 23.8-mile tour, *Bicycling Gettysburg National Military Park* (2019).

Maps to Bike Gettysburg No. 5 is the first mini-book in the series. It provides maps, GPS points, monument photos, and micro-histories for Route 5, "The Ridges Extended Loop," a 12.2-mile ride through the Gettysburg battlefield park. As its name suggests, it covers the main Confederate battle line on Seminary Ridge and the Union line on Cemetery Ridge. The loop is an extension of Route 4, "The Ridges Loop" and includes Devil's Den, Rose Woods, and The Peach Orchard. Both routes cover South Cavalry Field and Little Round Top. (With this mini-book, you can also cut-out 3.2 miles, effectively transitioning to Route 4).

My hope is that the *Maps to Bike Gettysburg* mini-book series will appeal to bicyclists who want short but detailed printed maps and bicycling directions for a variety of routes. Most bicyclists who enjoy learning history on two wheels will want to return to Gettysburg for many more rides. "Maps to Bike Gettysburg" gives you that option.

Gettysburg National Military Park

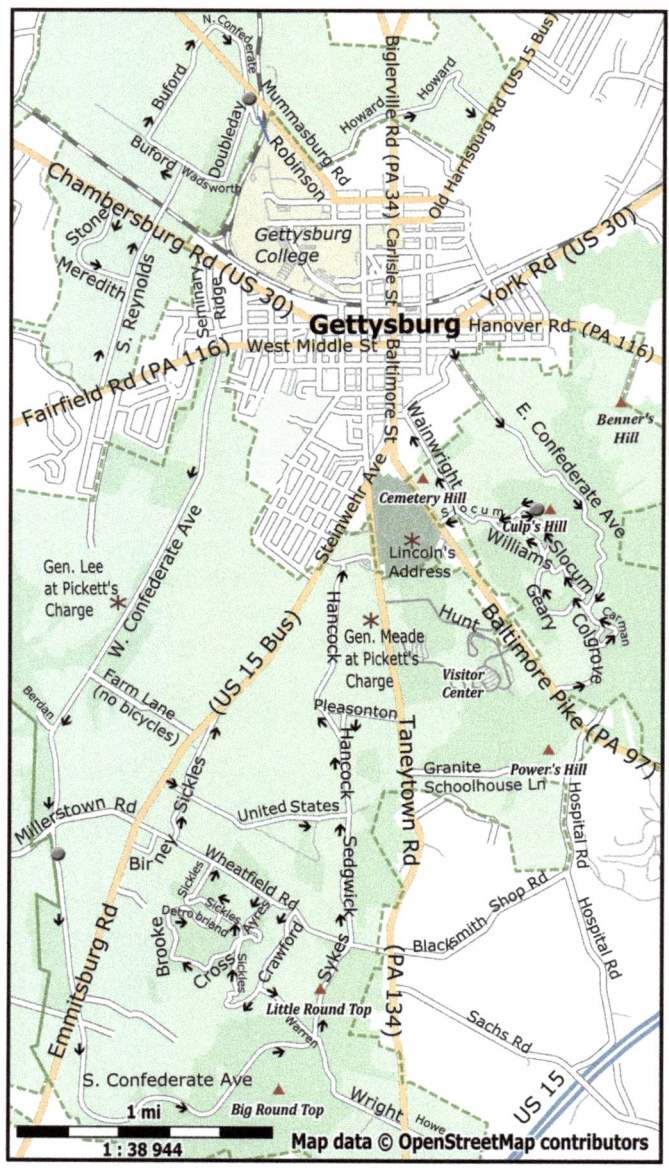

Map P.2. Gettysburg Park Roads

1.   Getting Your Mind In Gear

Many people feel a strong desire to visit and then return again to Gettysburg. We struggle to explain our connection to the land and the people who lived and died here. While exploring the battlefield park on two wheels, bicyclists know well the extraordinary feeling that Joshua Chamberlain described in 1889:

In great deeds something abides. On great fields something stays. Forms change and pass; bodies disappear, but spirits linger, to consecrate ground for the vision-place of souls. And reverent men and women from afar, and generations that know us not and that we know not of, heart-drawn to see where and by whom great things were suffered and done for them, shall come to this deathless field to ponder and dream... ~Col. Joshua Lawrence Chamberlain, "Dedication of the 20th Maine Monuments," October 3, 1889, Gettysburg.

This book will take you on a bicycle tour that allows the monuments and the Gettysburg landscape to teach you Civil War history. As a mini-book, it is deliberately brief and yet packed with color maps and turn-by-turn directions for a 12.2-mile bike ride. For a full educational experience, the reader is encouraged to consult Civil War Cycling's comprehensive guidebook, *Bicycling Gettysburg National Military Park.*

The Battle of Gettysburg (1863)

In 1863, Gen. Robert E. Lee and his Confederate Army of Northern Virginia invaded Pennsylvania through Maryland and bore down on Gettysburg from the north. To meet the threat, the newly promoted Maj.

Gettysburg National Military Park

Gen. George G. Meade rallied the Union Army of the Potomac and advanced toward Gettysburg from the south. About 170,000 soldiers converged on this farming town, home to roughly 2,400 citizens, ten miles north of the Maryland border. After three days of fighting on July 1–3, Lee's army was defeated but allowed to retreat back to Virginia. It was the deadliest battle in U.S. military history:

	Union	Confederate	Total
Dead:	3,155	3,903	7,058
Wounded:	14,529	18,735	33,264
Missing/Captured:	5,365	5,425	10,790
Total:	23,049	28,063	51,112

Table 1.1. Gettysburg Casualties

Source: American Battlefield Trust, battlefields.org/learn/civil-war/battles/gettysburg.

A Visual Summary of the Battle—Five Maps

The next five pages summarize the Battle of Gettysburg as a sequence of five military maps. These maps are *deliberately impressionistic* and designed for the overall purpose of learning on-the-go. (Please consult a military atlas if you require more detail).

Army-level battle lines have a blurred look to suggest approximate positions that a bicyclist can commit to memory without having to juggle the names of corps, divisions, or regiments. Union lines are blue and Confederate lines are red. Military positions overlay a modern road network so that bicyclists can easily orient themselves on the battlefield and also understand the high-level battle narrative in the context of one's current location.

July 1, 1863—Wednesday

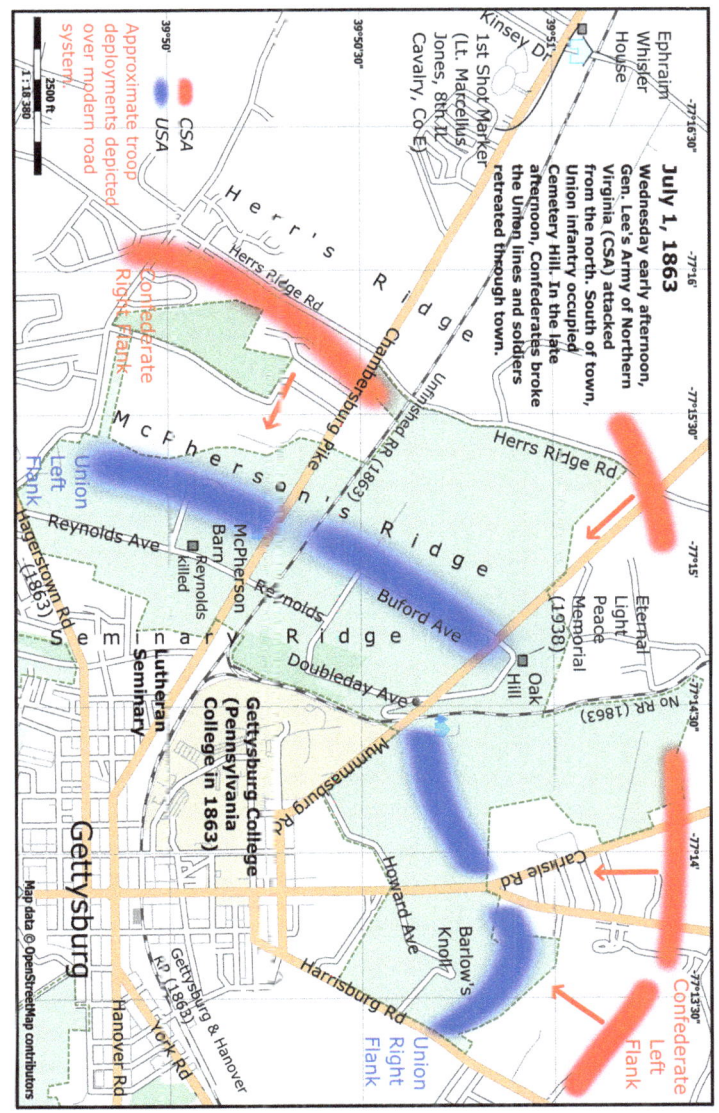

Map 1.1. July 1—Wednesday

Maps to Bike Gettysburg No. 5   15

Gettysburg National Military Park

July 2, 1863—Thursday

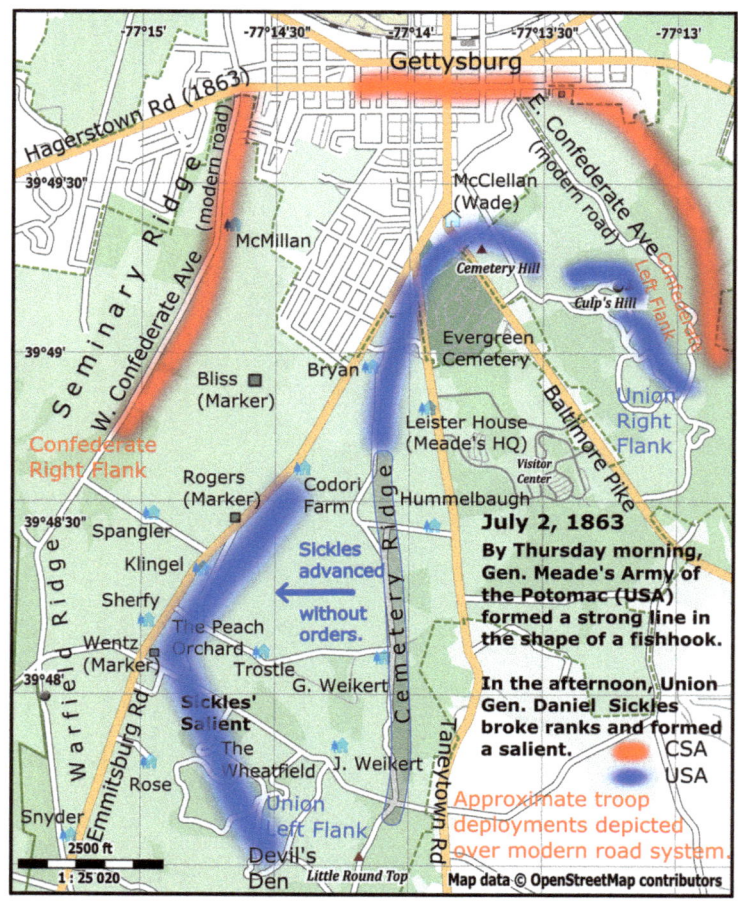

Map 1.2. July 2—Thursday Morning

While riding your bicycle through the Gettysburg battlefield, look for tall natural and physical structures (like Little Round Top or the Pennsylvania and Virginia State Monuments) to help you to stay oriented using this book's maps.

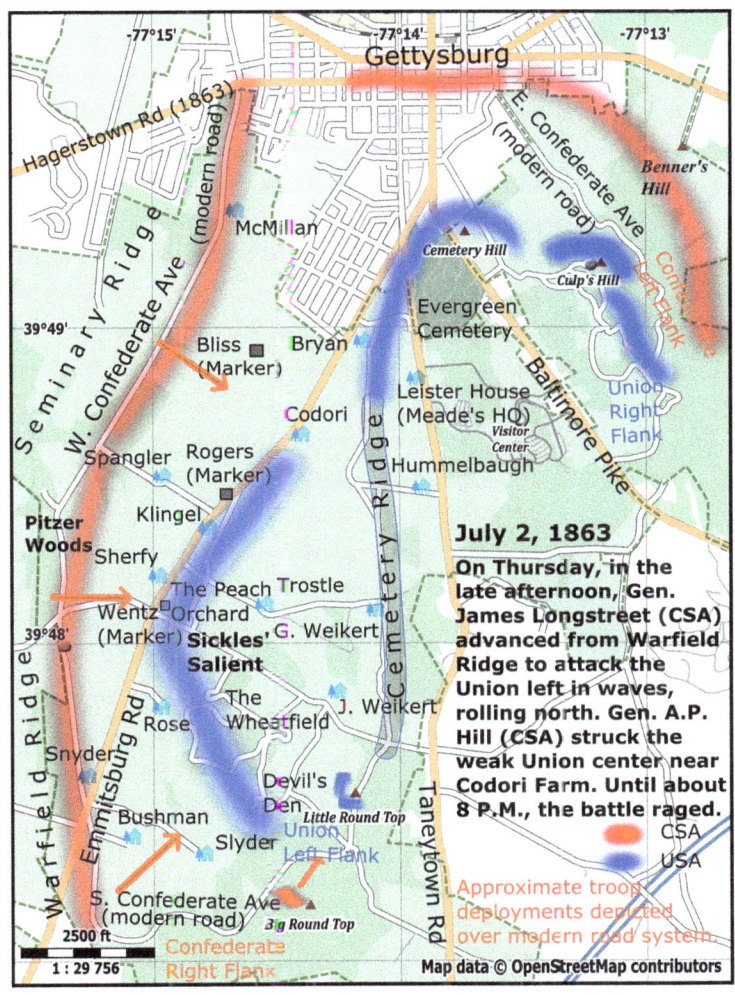

Map 1.3. July 2—Thursday Thursday Late Afternoon

Gettysburg barns have a distinctive shape, especially the three-steeple Codori barn. If you take the time to place them on a map, the battlefield story is easier to understand.

Maps to Bike Gettysburg No. 5   17

Gettysburg National Military Park

July 2 & 3, 1863—Battle for Culp's Hill

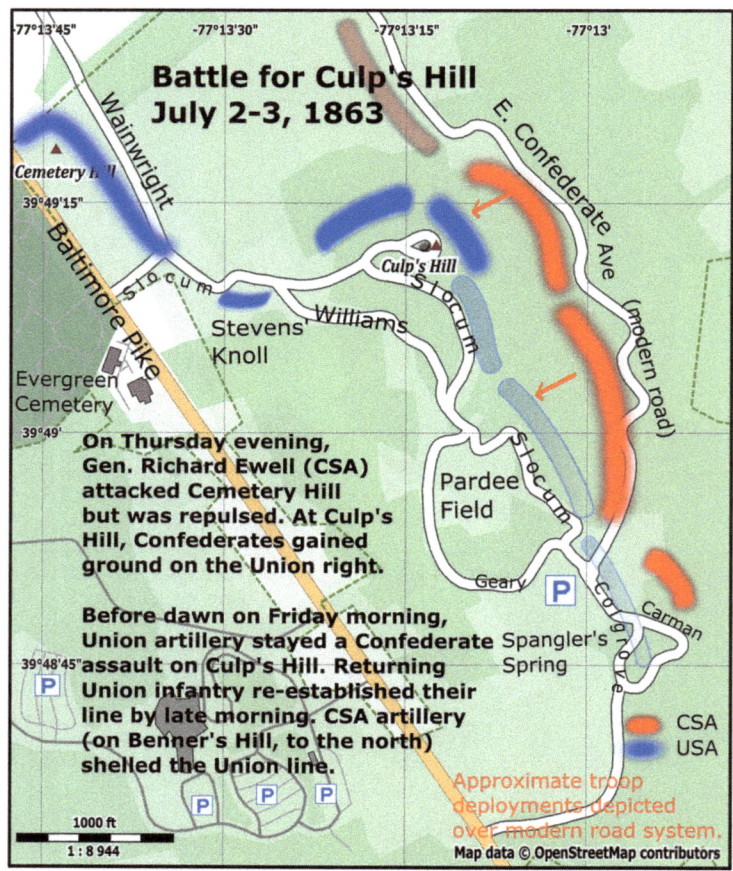

Map 1.4. July 2 and 3—Battle for Culp's Hill

Touring busses are not permitted in the Culp's Hill area (and not part of the official NPS auto tour). But for bicyclists, this much neglected tourist area offers a beautiful but relatively steep up and down ride. See Route 3 ("Battle Days 2 & 3") if you want a bicycle route that includes Culp's Hill.

July 3, 1863—Pickett's Charge

Map 1.5. July 3—Pickett's Charge

A walk in the fields of Pickett's Charge (the one-mile hike from Seminary to Cemetery Ridge) will broaden your understanding of the impact of geography on the results of the battle.

Gettysburg National Military Park

Gettysburg National Military Park

After the U.S. Civil War, former Union Maj. Gen. Daniel E. Sickles sponsored legislation to establish a national military park in Gettysburg, Pennsylvania. He introduced H.R. 8096 in 1894, and Congress approved the bill in 1895. Since that time, Gettysburg National Military Park has grown to more than 6,000 acres under the management of the National Park Service. For modern maps of park roads and geography, see Map P.2 on p. 12 and Map 1.6 on p. 21, respectively.

Today, most roads in Gettysburg National Military Park are named after Union officers of the Army of the Potomac. The shape of each park road roughly matches the battlefield formation for the soldiers under that officer's command. This park feature can be very helpful to bicyclists who want to understand the battlefield story relative to one's current location. For example, the broken and angled shape of Sickles Avenue depicts Sickles' tenuous 3rd Corps line on July 2, 1863. You can see this by matching Sickles' line shown on Map 1.3 with Sickles Avenue on Map P.2.

At Gettysburg, the NPS maintains more than 1,300 monuments and markers. There are eighteen state monuments on Seminary and Cemetery Ridges. Throughout the park stand eight large equestrian monuments (six Union and two Confederate generals) and many more bronze portrait statues. Most of Gettysburg's monuments are dedicated to regiments in the Army of the Potomac, although you will find many Confederate markers and cast-iron tablets.

Clearly, it is well beyond the scope of this mini-book to identify more than a small sampling of monuments that you will find while riding Route 5.

Map 1.6. Gettysburg Geography

Gettysburg National Military Park

The Ridges Extended Loop (No. 5)

Route 5, the "Ridges Extended Loop," is a 12.2-mile scenic ride along Seminary Ridge and Cemetery Ridge. It covers the main Confederate and Union battle lines for July 2 and 3, 1863. See Map 1.7, p.24.

Most Civil War Cycling routes begin and end at 945 Baltimore Pike, currently near a hotel and 0.5 miles north of the Gettysburg National Military Park (GNMP) Visitor Center. This location simplifies the design of safe, convenient, and circular routes that are composed of reusable segments (more on that, below). It is also close to the GNMP Bus/RV parking, where there are restrooms and water, and to Spangler's Spring parking. Your "on ramp" to the park is Baltimore Pike at Slocum Avenue.

We begin Route 5 by zigzagging through residential streets to ride south along Seminary Ridge and its southern extension, Warfield Ridge. Next, we ride east through South Cavalry Field. And finally, visit Little Round Top, Devil's Den, Rose Woods, and The Peach Orchard before riding north on Cemetery Ridge and back to our starting point. See Map 1.6 on p. 21, and Map 1.7 on p. 24.

Understanding Segment Maps

Route 5 is one of fourteen Gettysburg bicycling routes published by Civil War Cycling. Each route is designed by chaining together a series of "segments" that function as "building blocks" for creating routes. Although Route 1 consists of Segments A through L, in order, other routes contain a different number and ordering of segments. Route 5 consists of seven segments (A, F, G, H, J, K, and L) that total 12.2 miles:

Segment A	1.6 miles
Segment F	3.3 miles
Segment G	1.4 miles
Segment H	2.6 miles
Segment J	1.4 miles
Segment K	0.8 miles
Segment L	1.1 miles
Total:	12.2 miles

The odometer readings in this book are accurate to +/- 0.05 mile but can vary based on your riding style and equipment. Also, detailed directions in the form of cue tables will help confirm your location on the battlefield.

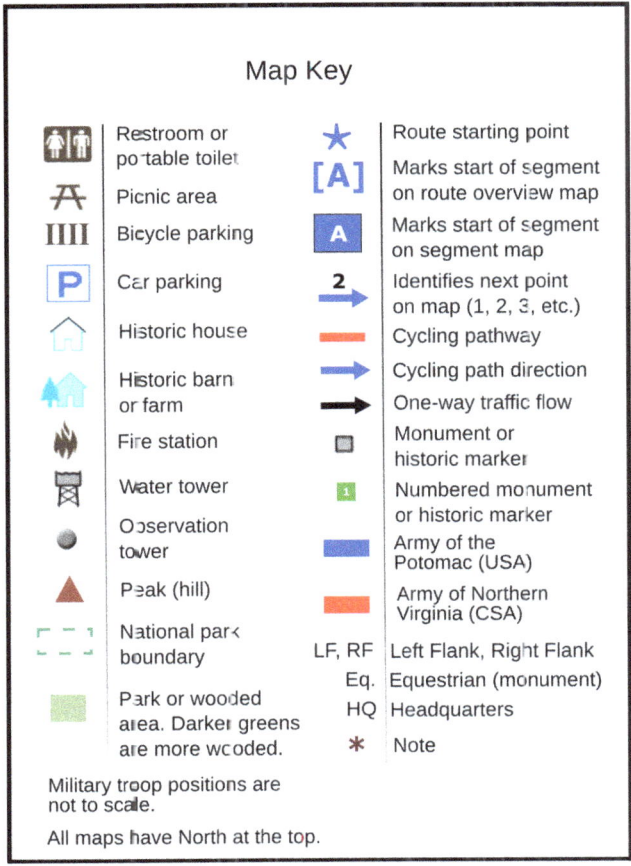

Table 1.2. Map and Symbol Key

Gettysburg National Military Park

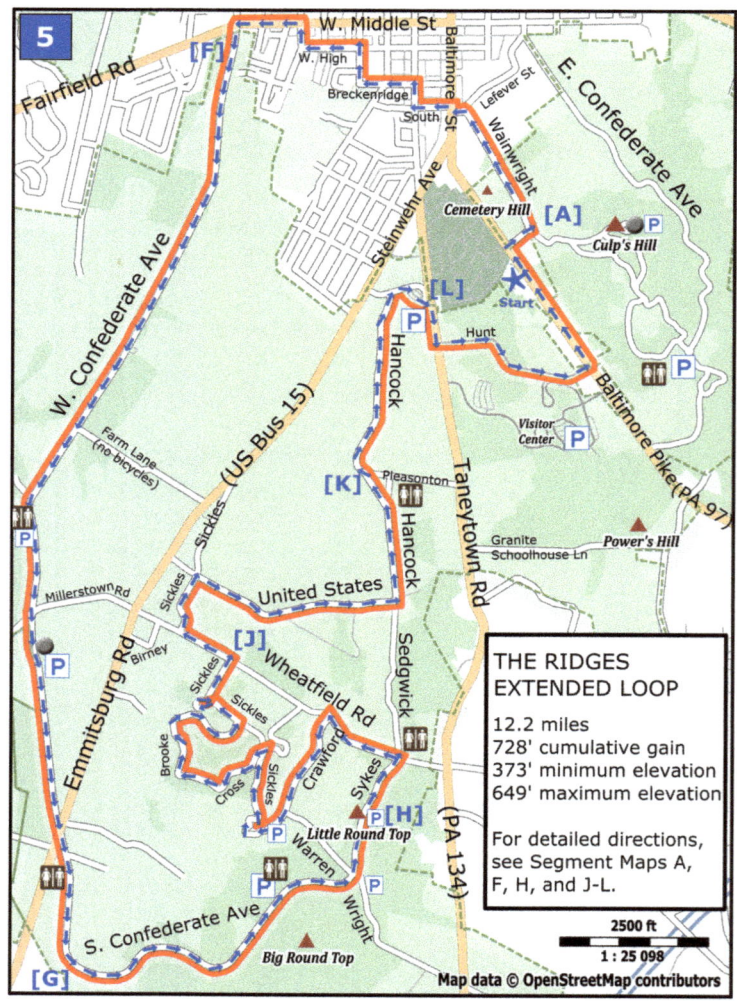

Map 1.7. Route 5 Overview Map

Maps, turn-by-turn directions, and monument highlights for each segment follow. Tip: To cut out 3.2 miles, head north on Sedgwick Ave. early in Segment H, effectively transitioning to Route 4 (9.0 total miles).

Understanding Bicycle Cues

Bicycle "cues" are short instructions for completing a route. Each segment map has a corresponding cue table that may use these abbreviations:

◀L	Turn Left	R▶	Turn Right
◀QL	Quick Left	QR▶	Quick Right
◀BL	Bear Left	BR▶	Bear Right
PoL	Pass on Left	PoR	Pass on Right
CS	Continue Straight	ST	Straight Through
SS	Stop Sign	TL	Traffic Light
X	Cross	U	U-Turn
DE	Dead-End	T	T Intersection
UM	Un-Marked	Y	Y Intersection
RR	Railroad	b/c	Becomes
N	North	E	East
S	South	W	West

Table 1.3. Bicycle Cue Abbreviations

Park road signs are often not located or visible at a point at which bicyclists need to make a turning decision. They are black cast iron signs that lie close to the ground. Refer to the maps and cue tables for help. Also, route detours (if any) are highlighted in gray and optionally replace the previous listed instruction.

Finding Battlefield Monuments

Segment maps have white-on-green numbers that identify a small number of featured monuments. For detailed coverage and photos of 100+ monuments, see the guidebook, *Bicycling Gettysburg National Military Park*. You can use both books together but for different purposes. For example, you could read the guidebook before your trip and carry this mini-book on your ride.

Gettysburg National Military Park

Park Bicycling Policies & Town Ordinances

The road network at Gettysburg National Military Park is designed to keep motor vehicles moving in one direction, which means there are many one-way roads. This can be a problem for bicyclists, since not having a pre-planned route can result in feeling frustrated at having to ride many miles to get to a point only a few hundred yards away. Fortunately, if you use Civil War Cycling's maps and directions, you can ride a loop that follows one-way signs. It is worth noting, however, that GNMP policies explicitly allow bicyclists to ride against the flow of traffic within the park (see Section 36, CFR 4.30, *Superintendent's Compendium*, 2016). But not everyone wants to risk confusing motor vehicle drivers.

As for sidewalks in downtown Gettysburg, bicyclists may ride on sidewalks, unless posted otherwise, but they must yield to pedestrians (Code 3-106). Please note that although Gettysburg is a relatively small town, motor vehicle traffic is often congested and bicycle lanes are rare. Even if you are an expert road cyclist, for example, the approach to the Lutheran Seminary while riding on West Middle Street can be dangerous due to fast-moving truck traffic on this steep hill with no bicycle lane (but there is a sidewalk). The maps in this book will identify sidewalk options for your consideration.

At the Gettysburg Museum & Visitor Center, "riders should walk their bikes while on pedestrian walks and trails." Not surprisingly, off-road riding is prohibited (www.nps.gov/gett/planyourvisit) in GNMP. You may walk your bicycle at the national cemetery. And finally, check the "Alerts & Conditions" page on the park website before your ride; this site is regularly updated: https://www.nps.gov/gett/planyourvisit/conditions.htm.

2. Let's Go! Bike Route 5

Route 5 Synopsis

Difficulty	Easy (for most healthy tourists)
Time	3 hours (frequent stops)
Distance	12.2 miles
Cumulative Gain	728 feet
Historical Focus	Battle of Gettysburg Days 2 & 3
Geography	East Cemetery Hill, Seminary Ridge, Little Round Top, Devil's Den, Rose Woods, The Peach Orchard, and Cemetery Ridge
Safety	Mostly 25 mph park roads (1.1 miles on residential streets)

Similarities Between Routes 3–5

Routes 3, 4, and 5 are among the most popular of Civil War Cycling's options for self-directed bike tours through Gettysburg National Military Park. One reason is that they cover modest distances (17.0, 9.0, and 12.2 miles, respectively). But also, these three routes omit a tour of the northern half of the battlefield, which significantly reduces any need to ride on public roads. Instead, Routes 3, 4, and 5 privilege the southern half of the battlefield, where there is far more opportunity to enjoy the tree-lined park avenues that weave through Gettysburg's most famous geographic landmarks.

For a shorter ride totaling 9.0 miles, Route 4 ("The Ridges Loop") drops coverage of Devil's Den, Rose Woods, and the Trostle Farm area. For a longer ride of 17.0 miles, you may want to consider Route 3 ("Battle Days 2 & 3") to add a complete tour of Culp's Hill.

Gettysburg National Military Park

Segment A (East Cemetery Hill)

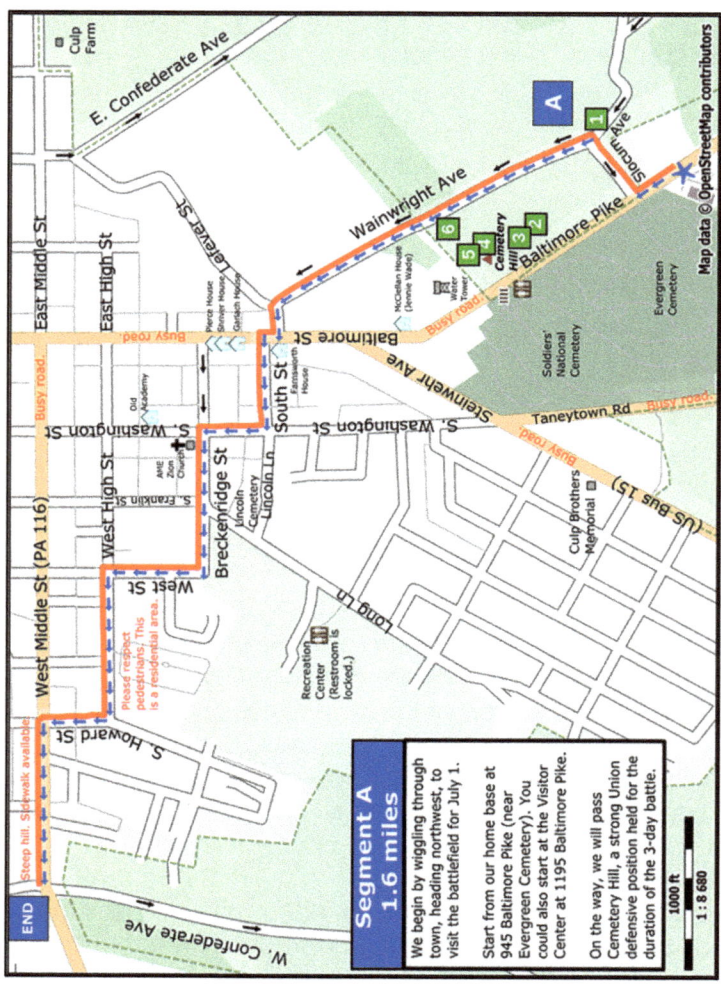

Map 2.1. Route 5 Segment A (1.6 miles)

Remember: White-on-green numbers identify monuments whose photos are on the following pages.

28   The Ridges Extended Loop

Segment A Cues (1.6 miles)

From 945 Baltimore Pike to north end of W. Confederate Avenue:		Seg	Total
0.0	RIGHT on Slocum (400 feet against traffic)	0.1	**0.1**
0.1	LEFT on Wainwright to tour East Cemetery Hill, to stop sign at Lefever	0.5	**0.5**
0.5	LEFT at Lefever to Baltimore. CROSS to sidewalk	0.5	**0.5**
	RIGHT onto sidewalk, then quick LEFT on South for 1 block	0.7	**0.7**
0.7	RIGHT on S. Washington for 1 block to Breckenridge	0.8	**0.8**
0.8	LEFT on Breckenridge to dead-end at West	1.0	**1.0**
1.0	RIGHT on West for 1 block to stop sign at W. High	1.1	**1.1**
1.1	LEFT on W. High to dead-end on Howard	1.3	**1.3**
1.3	RIGHT on Howard for 1 block	1.4	**1.4**
1.4	CROSS W. Middle to sidewalk and then LEFT up steep hill to traffic light	1.6	**1.6**

Table 2.1. Segment A Cues

Segment A Monument Highlights

For each route segment, this book provides photos and short descriptions for a sampling of monuments. Numbers on the map match-up to photo numbers. GPS coordinates (lat, lon) are listed above each photo.

Gettysburg National Military Park

1. 39.81990, -77.22617

2. 39.82098, -77.22875

3. 39.82132, -77.22889

4. 39.82165, -77.22888

5. 39.82195, -77.22888

6. 39.82264, -77.22811

The Ridges Extended Loop

1. 33rd Massachusetts Monument (1885)

With the 5th Maine Artillery Battery, the 33rd Massachusetts decimated the 57th North Carolina as they came at them from the east, and while the Louisiana Tigers fired upon them from the north.

2. 4th Ohio Monument (1887)

According to the monument inscription, the 4th Ohio was "hotly engaged in support of batteries on East Cemetery Hill until after 10 P.M." on July 2, 1863.

3. Winfield Hancock Equestrian Monument (1895-6)

Winfield Scott Hancock, nicknamed "Hancock the Superb," was a Pennsylvania native. He commanded the 2nd Corps of the Army of the Potomac, and was wounded southwest of here, during Pickett's Charge.

4. Oliver O. Howard Headquarters Monument

Maj. Gen. Howard established his headquarters on the high ground of East Cemetery Hill after ceding the town to the Army of Northern Virginia on July 1.

5. Oliver O. Howard Equestrian Monument (1932)

Oliver Otis Howard was from Maine. He commanded the 11th Corps of the Army of the Potomac, a group of mostly German immigrants.

6. 17th Connecticut Monument (1889)

On July 1, after retreating south from Barlow's Knoll, the 17th Connecticut fought here on East Cemetery Hill. Their commander, Lt. Col. Douglas Fowler, died from artillery fire while riding his white horse on the knoll.

Gettysburg National Military Park

Segment F (Seminary Ridge)

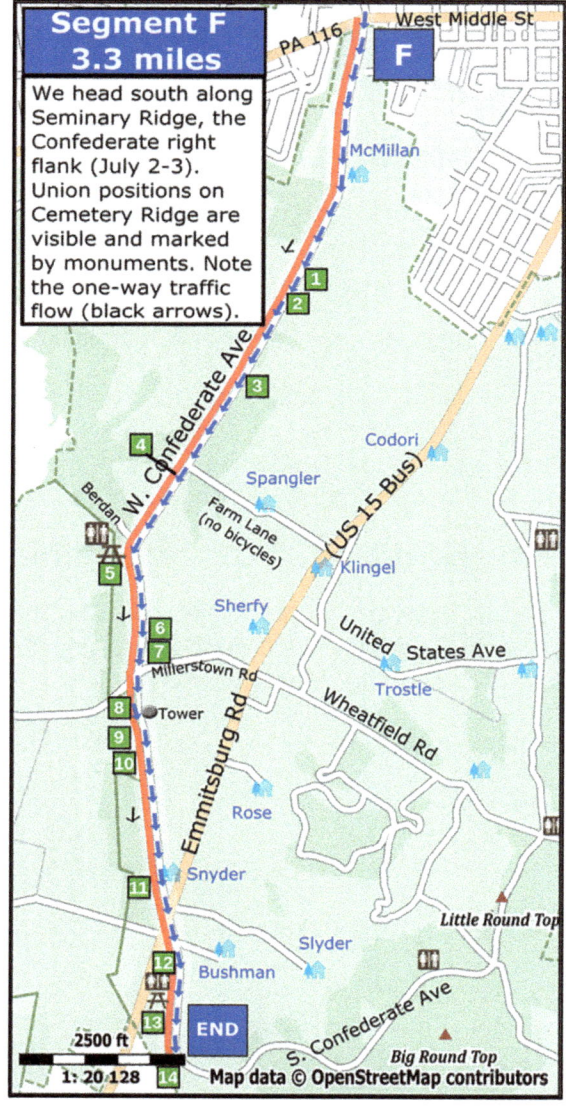

Map 2.2. Route 5 Segment F (3.3 miles)

Segment F Cues (3.3 miles)

South on W. Confederate to Soldiers and Sailors Monument:		Seg	Total
0.0	From W. Middle, LEFT at light onto W. Confederate (riding south) for 0.1 miles	1.1	**2.7**
1.1	At Virginia State Monument, continue straight to Amphitheater for 0.8 miles	1.9	**3.5**
1.9	Continue straight to Millerstown Road for 0.3 miles	2.2	**3.8**
2.2	CROSS Millerstown, then straight to Longstreet Observation Tower for 0.1 miles	2.3	**3.9**
2.3	Continue straight to Emmitsburg Road for 0.5 miles	2.8	**4.4**
2.8	CROSS Emmitsburg at S. Confederate to picnic area for 0.2 miles	3.0	**4.6**
3.0	Continue straight to Soldiers and Sailors Monument for 0.3 miles	3.3	**4.9**

Table 2.2. Segment F Cues

Segment F Monument Highlights

1. 39.81833, -77.24725

2. 39.81769, -77.24803

Maps to Bike Gettysburg No. 5

Gettysburg National Military Park

Segment F is a mostly flat ride along Seminary Ridge.

3. 39.81422, -77.25036

4. 39.81008, -77.25397

5. 39.80572, -77.25656

6. 39.80300, -77.25586

7. 39.80243, -77.25586

8. 39.80002, -77.25638

1. North Carolina State Monument (1929)

The North Carolina State Monument faces east toward Union positions on Cemetery Ridge. From this location, Pettigrew's brigade joined Pickett's Charge.

2. Tennessee State Monument (1982)

This monument honors three regiments in Archer's brigade. It was the last Confederate state monument erected at Gettysburg.

3. Virginia State Monument (1917)

Virginia erected the first Confederate state monument at Gettysburg. It is the largest and most expensive Confederate monument in the park.

4. Florida State Monument (1963)

The three stars on the Florida State Monument represent the three regiments of Perry's brigade.

5 & 8. Longstreet Equestrian & HQ Monuments

James Longstreet commanded Lee's 1st corps. His 1998 equestrian monument by Gary Casteel is the first anywhere dedicated to him.

6. Louisiana State Monument (1971)

This monument depicts an iconic female figure hovering over a wounded Louisiana artilleryman.

7. Mississippi State Monument (1973)

This monument depicts a fallen color bearer and a Confederate soldier. It marks where Barksdale's brigade began its charge through The Peach Orchard.

Gettysburg National Military Park

Segment F covers the main Confederate battle line.

9. 39.79889, -77.25592

10. 39.79792, -77.25583

11. 39.79264, -77.25508

12. 39.78997, -77.25428

13. 39.78658, -77.25422

14. 39.78499, -77.25404

The Ridges Extended Loop

9. Georgia State Monument (1961)

The Georgia State Monument bears this haunting inscription: "We Sleep Here in Obedience to Law. When Duty Called, We Came. When Country Called, We Died." Semmes' brigade was positioned here on July 2.

10. South Carolina State Monument (1963)

This monument honors South Carolinians who had an "abiding faith in the sacredness of States Rights." It marks the location where Kershaw's brigade initiated its attack through The Peach Orchard on July 2.

11. Arkansas State Monument (1966)

From this spot, the 3rd Arkansas joined Robertson's Texas brigade to attack the Union left on July 2, ultimately fighting in Devil's Den.

12. Texas State Monument (1964)

Robertson's Texas brigade fell back to this position after its attack on Little Round Top and Devil's Den. A simple Lone Star adorns the monument.

13. Alabama State Monument (1933)

From near this location on July 2, Law's Alabama brigade launched its assault on Little Round Top. The United Daughters of the Confederacy secured funding for the Alabama State Monument.

14. Soldiers and Sailors Monument (1965)

This monument was dedicated in honor of the service of all Confederate military personnel, in all battles but especially Gettysburg.

Gettysburg National Military Park

Near the modern-day Virginia State Monument, you can see the fields of "Pickett's Charge":

This view from the North Carolina State Monument shows the south end of the ridge at the Round Tops:

On July 2, Little Round Top became a major target for Confederate Lt. Gen. Longstreet's assault on the Union left. Here from the Longstreet Observation Tower, we see Little Round Top on the left and Big Round on the right. The Lewis Bushman farm buildings are located on the west side of the ridge.

The next photo shows the 4th New York Independent Battery monument in Devil's Den. Little Round Top is in the background.

Gettysburg National Military Park

Segment G (Little Round Top)

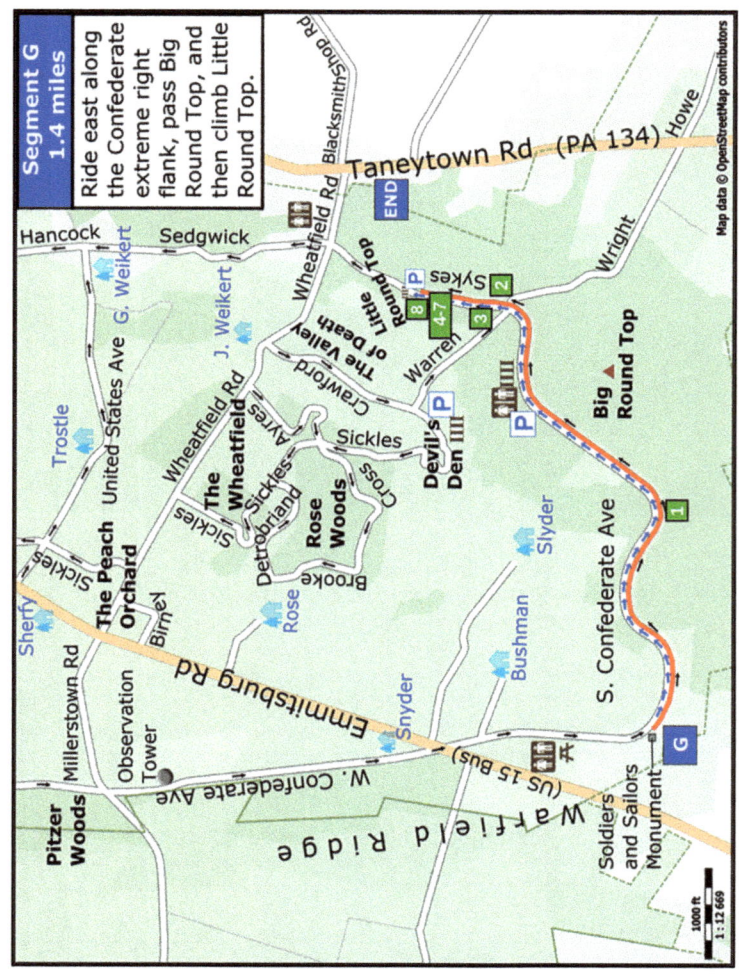

Map 2.3. Route 5 Segment G (1.4 miles)

Segment G starts as a pleasant downhill ride, shifts to a gradual incline, and then ends with a steep climb up Sykes Avenue to Little Round Top.

Segment G Cues (1.4 miles)

Soldiers and Sailors Monument to Little Round Top:		Seg	Total
0.0	From Soldiers and Sailors Monument, continue straight (east) for 0.5 miles	0.5	**5.4**
0.5	CROSS Plum Run, then uphill for 0.4 miles to Big Round Top parking lot	0.9	**5.8**
0.9	At Big Round Top parking lot, straight for 0.3 miles to first (confusing) intersection	1.2	**6.1**
1.2	STRAIGHT at intersection onto Sykes for 0.2 miles to Little Round Top parking lot	1.4	**6.3**

Table 2.3. Segment G Cues

Segment G Monument Highlights

Enjoy the rest after having conquered a few challenging hills. Lock your bicycle in the Little Round Top parking lot, then find monuments 2–8 on foot.

1. 39.78486, -77.24564

2. 39.78947, -77.23617

Gettysburg National Military Park

Segment G covers the Confederate trek to attack the Union left flank at Little Round Top.

3. 39.79095, -77.23710

4. 39.79095, -77.23711

5. 39.79127, -77.23713

6. 39.79144, -77.23703

7. 39.79217, -77.23672

8. 39.79253, -77.23667

The Ridges Extended Loop

1. William W. Wells Statue (1913)

Major Wells was awarded the Medal of Honor for his role in Farnsworth's cavalry charge on July 3.

2. 20th Maine Monument (1889)

Joshua Chamberlain's regiment held the Union left flank against the 15th Alabama on Little Round Top.

3. 83rd Pennsylvania Monument (1889)

This regiment's brigade commander, Strong Vincent, rallied soldiers to defend Little Round Top.

4. Strong Vincent Wounded Monument (1878, 1978)

Beyond the national cemetery, this is Gettysburg's oldest marker for a mortally wounded soldier.

5. 44th and 12th New York Monument (1893)

This "castle" monument is the largest and most expensive regimental monument at Gettysburg.

6. 140th New York Monument (1889)

This monument stands near where its commander, Irish immigrant Patrick O'Rorke, died on July 2.

7. 91st Pennsylvania Monument (1889)

The Maltese cross on the top of this monument identifies Sykes' 5th corps.

8. Gouverneur K. Warren Statue (1888)

Army Chief Engineer Warren mobilized the 5th Corps to defend Little Round Top.

Gettysburg National Military Park

Segment H (Devil's Den)

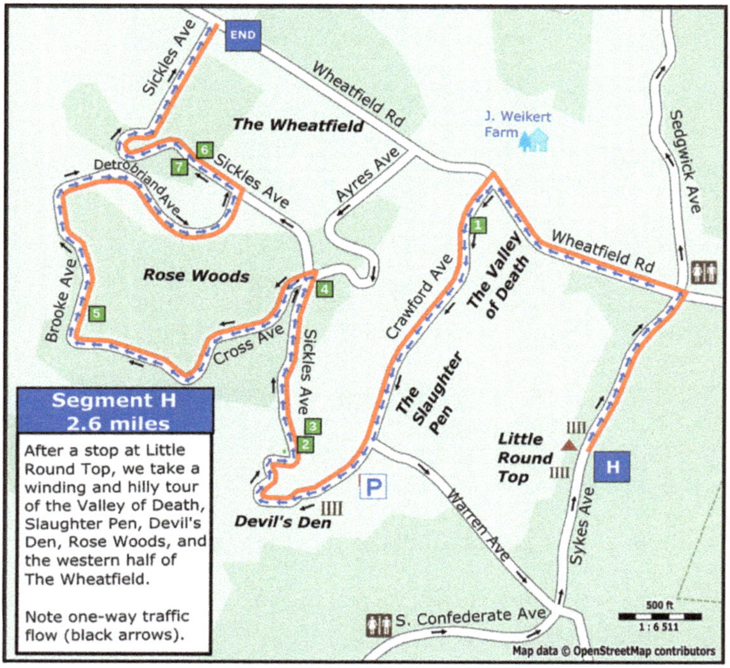

Map 2.4. Route 5 Segment H (2.6 miles)

This is a view of Devil's Den while looking southwest (over "The Slaughter Pen") from Little Round Top. Warfield Ridge is in the mid-distance.

The Ridges Extended Loop

Segment H Cues (2.6 miles)

Little Round Top to Devil's Den and Rose Woods:	Seg	Total
0.0 From Little Round Top parking lot, ride north (downhill) on Sykes 0.3 miles to stop	0.3	**6.6**
0.3 LEFT on Wheatfield, downhill for 0.3 miles to Crawford	0.6	**6.9**
0.6 LEFT on Crawford for 0.3 miles to stop sign at Warren and Sickles	0.9	**7.2**
0.9 Straight into Devil's Den parking lot, and up steep hill to large Oak tree, 0.3 miles	1.2	**7.5**
1.2 Straight into Rose Woods to first (confusing) intersection	1.4	**7.7**
1.4 Hard LEFT on unmarked Cross (becomes Brooke then Detrobriand), 0.8 miles	2.2	**8.5**
2.2 LEFT on Sickles at dead-end, following to stop sign at Wheatfield Road, 0.4 miles	2.6	**8.9**

Table 2.4. Segment H Cues

Segment H Monument Highlights

1. 39.79597, -77.23875   **2.** 39.79201, -77.24252

Gettysburg National Military Park

3. 39.79217, -77.23672

4. 39.79494, -77.24190

5. 39.79484, -77.24685

6. 39.79718, -77.24500

7. 39.79703, -77.24511

Sickles Avenue winds around Devil's Den, where about 200 million years ago, dinosaurs roamed this basin. On the south side of the boulder outcropping, the avenue snakes up to a large oak "witness tree." At the top of this short road, we enter Rose Woods for a shady up and down ride.

1. Samuel W. Crawford Statue (1988)

Crawford's 3rd division fought at the base of Little Round Top in an area called The Valley of Death.

2. 4th New York Battery Monument (1888)

"Smith's Battery" anchored the Union 3rd Corps left flank in Devil's Den, and lost four guns to Texans who fought for Hood's Confederate division.

3. 99th Pennsylvania Monument (1889)

The diamond at the top of this monument identifies Maj. Gen. Sickles' 3rd Corps, Army of the Potomac.

4. 5th New Hampshire Monument (1886)

At this spot in Rose Woods, Col. Edward E. Cross fell mortally wounded on July 2. The four boulders at the monument base are from the Gettysburg battlefield.

5. 2nd Delaware Monument (1886, relocated 1909)

Here in Rose Woods, the 2nd Delaware fought Kershaw's South Carolinian brigade.

6. 5th Michigan Monument (1888-9)

This monument is located north of Detrobriand Avenue, a road named for brigade commander and French immigrant Col. P. Regis De Trobriand.

7. New York Irish Brigade Monument (1888)

This monument honors three regiments led by Col. Patrick Kelly. It is one of two Gettysburg monuments that feature the sculpture of a regimental dog; the other is the 11th Pennsylvania Monument on Oak Ridge.

Gettysburg National Military Park

Segment J (The Peach Orchard)

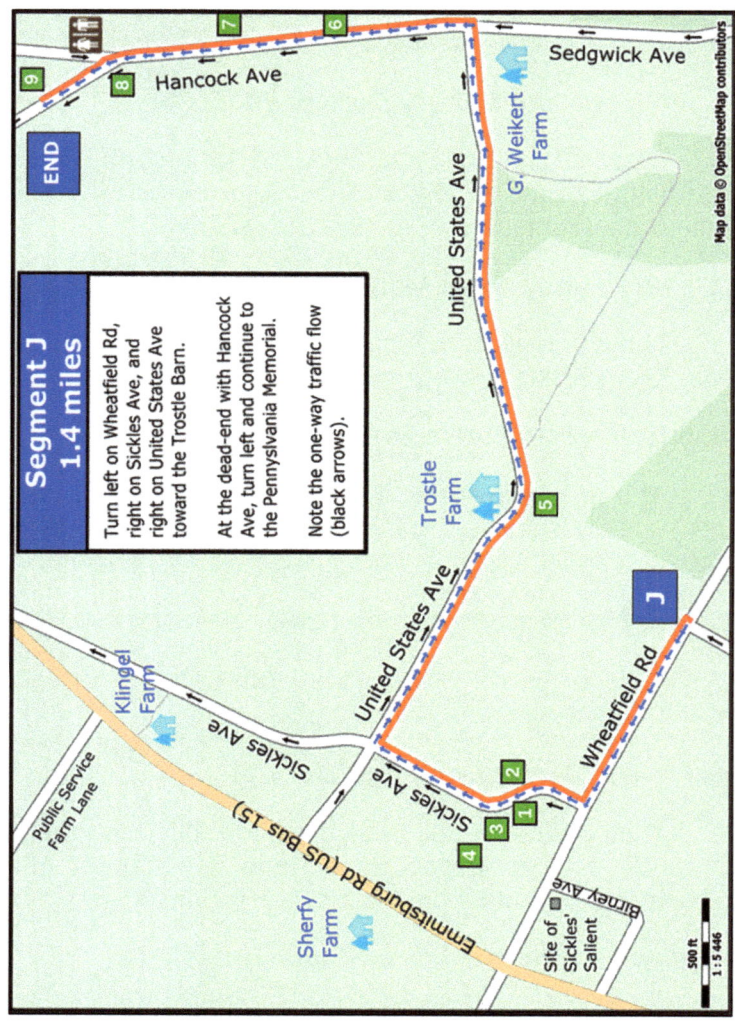

Map 2.5. Route 5 Segment J (1.4 miles)

(While riding, note how elevation impacts visibility).

48 The Ridges Extended Loop

Segment J Cues (1.4 miles)

Through Part of The Peach Orchard to Cemetery Ridge:		Seg	Total
0.0	From Sickles at Wheatfield Road, LEFT toward The Peach Orchard	0.0	**8.9**
	RIGHT at first road (still Sickles) to stop sign at United States, 0.2 miles	0.2	**9.1**
0.2	RIGHT on United States to dead-end at Hancock, 0.8 miles	1.0	**9.9**
1.0	LEFT on Hancock for 0.4 miles to parking near the Pennsylvania State Monument	1.4	**10.3**

Table 2.5. Segment J Cues

Segment J Monument Highlights

1. 39.80134, -77.24724   **2.** 39.80151, -77.24679

Rev. Joseph and Mary Sherfy owned this farmland along Emmitsburg Road, which included a peach orchard. Everything was destroyed on July 2, 1863.

Gettysburg National Military Park

3. 39.80180, -77.24750

4. 39.80208, -77.24814

5. 39.80187, -77.24303

6. 39.80345, -77.23436

7. 39.80420, -77.23441

8. 39.80662, -77.23505

The Confederate attack east through The Peach Orchard extended to Cemetery Ridge.

9. 39.80761, -77.23525

About 23,400 men from Pennsylvania fought at the Battle of Gettysburg. The 90 bronze tablets installed around the state monument list 44,500 Pennsylvanians who fought in the Civil War.

1. 1st New Jersey Light Artillery Monument, "Clark's Battery" B (1888)

This monument marks the position of Clark's artillery battery on July 2 while defending the Sherfy Peach Orchard from Confederate attack. Barksdale's Mississippi brigade attacked and forced this New Jersey unit to withdraw.

2. 7th New Jersey Monument (1888)

The 7th New Jersey Monument is shaped like a minié ball, a type of ammunition that was designed by Claude-Étienne Minié.

3. New York Excelsior Brigade Monument (1893)

The Excelsior monument honors the 2nd brigade of A. A. Humphreys' division, which was recruited by NYC politician turned soldier and later U.S. congressman, Daniel Sickles.

4. 73rd New York Monument (1897)

At the start of the U.S. Civil War, Michael Burns recruited firefighters to form Company A, 73rd New York. Barksdale's Mississippians hit this regiment at

The Peach Orchard and forced their retreat to Cemetery Ridge.

5. Daniel E. Sickles Headquarters Monument

Sickles commanded the Union 3rd Corps. He established his headquarters on Trostle Farm, where he was wounded by cannon fire on July 2. Surgeons amputated Sickles' right leg at a field hospital.

6. Rev. William Corby Statue (1910)

The future president of the University of Notre Dame, Rev. William Corby, was the chaplain of the Irish Brigade. His bronze statue is on Hancock Avenue.

7. New York State Auxiliary Monument (1925)

New York State erected this monument "in recognition of the services rendered by those corps, division and brigade commanders at Gettysburg not elsewhere honored on this field" (from its inscription).

8. 1st Minnesota Monument (1897)

This monument depicts the regiment's sacrificial charge led by Col. William Colvill on July 2 after Hancock ordered Colvill to "Take those colors!" This small regiment slammed into Lt. Gen. A. P. Hill's Confederates to stop the charge.

9. Pennsylvania State Monument (1910)

This is the largest and most expensive memorial in Gettysburg National Military Park. At its top is Samuel A. Murray's sculpture of the Goddess of Victory and Peace, which he created from about 7,500 pounds of melted civil war cannons. Eight bronze statues are installed around the structure.

The following photo shows the view from Seminary Ridge, overlooking part of the Sherfy farm. The monuments in the distance stand on Cemetery Ridge.

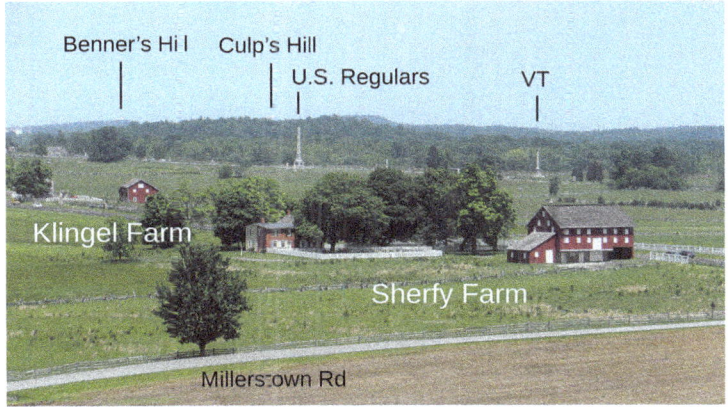

In the next segment, you will visit The Angle where Virginians breached the Union line during Pickett's Charge. The tree in this photo marks the spot:

Maps to Bike Gettysburg No. 5

Gettysburg National Military Park

Segment K (Cemetery Ridge)

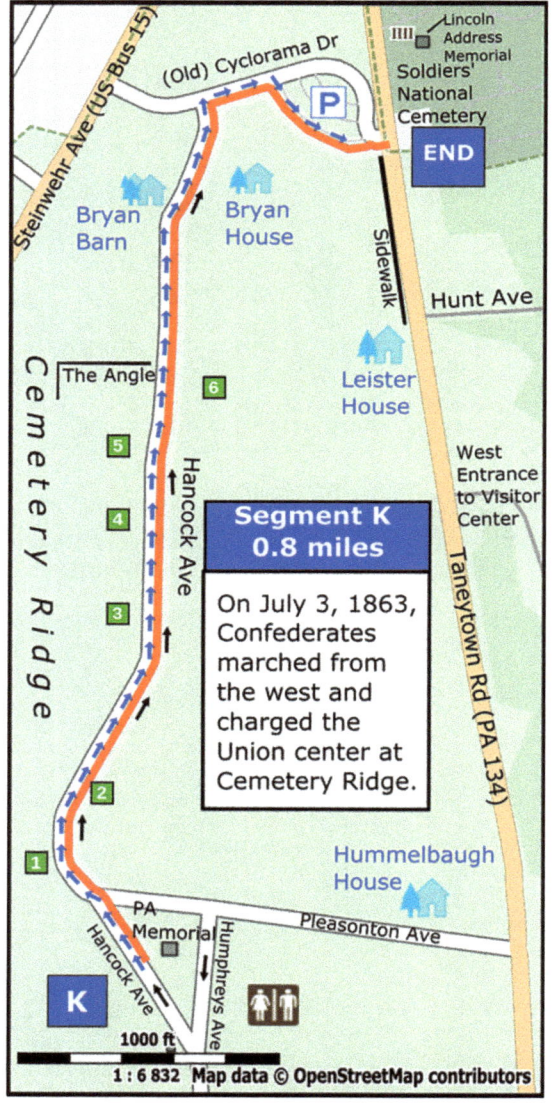

Map 2.6. Route 5 Segment K (0.8 miles)

Segment K Cues (0.8 miles)

Cemetery Ridge to Soldiers' National Cemetery Parking Lot:		Seg	Total
0.0	From the Pennsylvania State Monument, continue north for 0.6 miles to dead-end	0.6	**10.9**
0.6	RIGHT at dead-end and through parking lot to the Maryland State Monument, 0.8 miles	0.8	**11.1**

Table 2.6. Segment K Cues

1. 39.80876, -77.23705

2. 39.80942, -77.23650

1. Winfield S. Hancock Wounded Monument (1892)

During Pickett's Charge on July 3, Maj. Gen. Hancock was wounded in his right thigh near this location on Cemetery Ridge. He commanded the left wing of the Army of the Potomac.

2. Vermont State Monument (1889)

Vermont was the first state to erect a monument at Gettysburg. (In 2000, Delaware was the last).

Gettysburg National Military Park

3. 39.81124, -77.23575

4. 39.81246, -77.23570

5. 39.81319, -77.23587

6. 39.81397, -77.23492

3. U. S. Regulars Monument (1909)

Maj. Gen. George G. Meade's 95,000-man Army of the Potomac included over 7,000 federal ("Regular Army") soldiers, but most were volunteers from states.

4. High Water Mark, Copse of Trees (1892)

This monument's inscription honors the "patriotism and gallantry" of soldiers who repulsed Pickett's Charge on July 3. The trees are replanted versions of a copse on the battlefield ridge at the Union center.

The following photo was taken on the east side of Hancock Avenue (Cemetery Ridge), looking southwest over Emmitsburg Road toward the main Confederate battle line on Seminary Ridge. We are overlooking The Angle. South Mountain is in the distance.

The photo shows two very helpful landmarks for staying oriented on the Gettysburg battlefield. The first is the Codor Barn in the center of the photo. The barn is located on Emmitsburg Road, a road over which the Confederate army had to cross to attack the Union center line on July 3, 1863. Second, if you follow the road left (south), you can see the faint impression of the Longstreet Observation Tower at the end of Seminary Ridge. You may have noticed the tower while riding through The Peach Orchard in Segment J.

The civil war era cannons that you see mark the positions of three artillery batteries: the Rhode Island Battery A (whose clover-topped monument is the rightmost monument in the photo), and also two artillery batteries from New York. You will want to walk your bike for at least the north half of Hancock Avenue, because this area is densely monumented—and there are many wayside exhibits to study.

Gettysburg National Military Park

Segment L (Return)

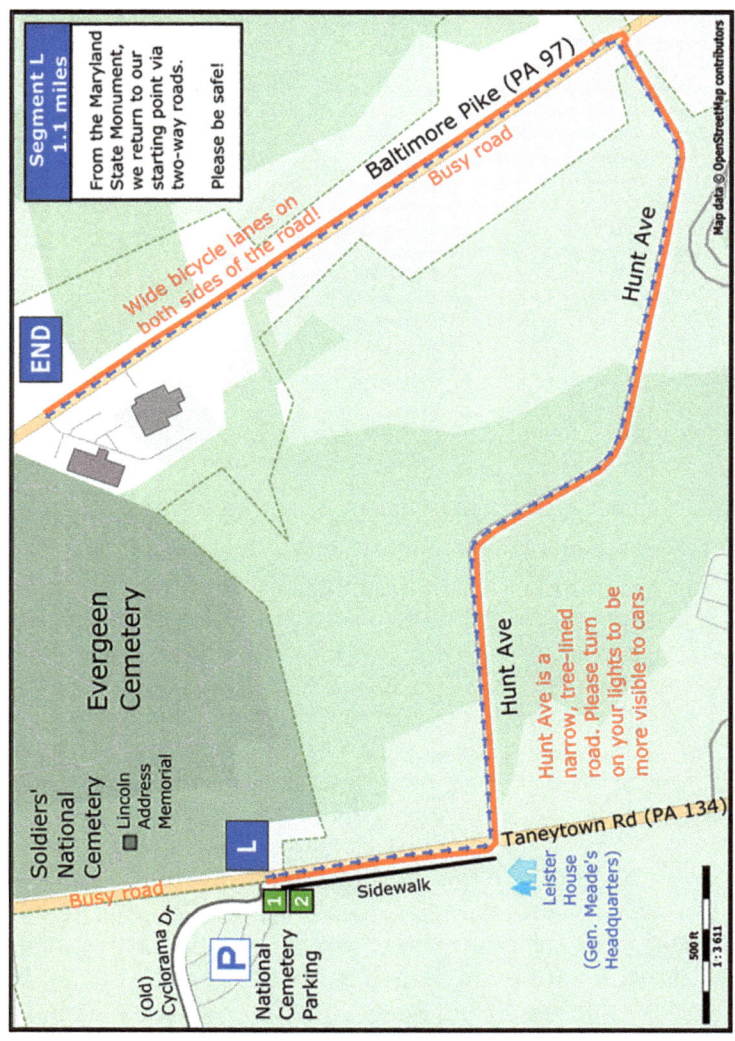

Map 2.7. Route 5 Segment L (1.1 miles)

Segment L Cues (1.1 miles)

Soldiers' National Cemetery Parking Lot Back to 945 Baltimore Pike:		Seg	Total
0.0	From Maryland State Monument, walk bike right (south) on sidewalk		**11.1**
	Follow Taneytown sidewalk to crosswalk at Hunt	0.1	**11.2**
0.1	CROSS Taneytown onto Hunt and continue to light at Baltimore Pike	0.7	**11.8**
0.7	LEFT on Baltimore Pike (wide shoulder for bicyclists) to starting point	1.1	**12.2**

Table 2.7. Segment L Cues

1. 39.81642, -77.23247   **2.** 39.81606, -77.23244

1. Maryland State Monument (1994)

The Maryland State Monument depicts a Union and Confederate soldier helping one another. Even though Maryland did not secede from the Union, men from Maryland fought in both armies at Gettysburg.

Gettysburg National Military Park

2. Delaware State Monument (2000)

This monument is dedicated to the Union and Confederate Delawareans who fought at Gettysburg.

Pass the monument and follow the sidewalk along Taneytown Road to the Lydia Leister property, Maj. Gen. Meade's army headquarters. (See the second photo, below). In the landscape photo, we are facing south toward Little Round Top. The Pennsylvania State Monument is mid-way down the ridge, in the distance.

3. What Next?

You did it! You cycled 12.2 miles along some of the most memorable portions of the Gettysburg battlefield. You learned about the Battle of Gettysburg while riding the gentle slope of Seminary Ridge; the hilly climb up to Little Round Top; and north along Cemetery Ridge.

I sincerely hope that you will want to return to Gettysburg and to explore more of its rich natural and physical landmarks, including more than 1,300 monuments and 400 refurbished Civil War cannons. In preparation for your next visit—or maybe to revive memories of your most recent ride—you will want to consult *Bicycling Gettysburg National Military Park: The Cyclist's Civil War Travel Guide*. This information-packed book describes a 23.8-mile tour of the entire park and includes numerous color photos of landmarks and historical monuments.

Guidebooks by Sue Thibodeau:

ISBN 9781732603806

286 pp, full-color
6"x9" perfect bound pbk

Published March 2019
by Civil War Cycling

www.civilwarcycling.com

Available for order at
your favorite book seller.

ISBN 9781732603813

208 pp, full-color
6"x9" perfect bound pbk

Published November
2020 by Civil War
Cycling

www.civilwarcycling.com

Available for order at
your favorite book seller.

Forthcoming Publications:

Bicycling Chickamauga Battlefield (2021)

Bicycling Shiloh National Military Park (2022)

www.ingramcontent.com/pod-product-compliance
Lightning Source LLC
Chambersburg PA
CBHW042121100526
44587CB00025B/4141